The
Landa List

Grammar Guidelines,
Punctuation Principles,
and
Proofreading Practices

David Hatcher and Lane Goddard

For additional copies (and other useful books) go to www.landabooks.com.

Landa Books

Tools & TRAINING
for everyday writers & their teachers

ISBN 1-57420-001-1

Third Edition

97 96 95 94   10 9 8 7 6 5

Chatelaine Press
6454 Honey Tree Court
Burke, VA 22015
800-249-9527
http://www.chatpress.com

The Landa List

Contents

Section 1 Punctuation

Apostrophes

A good tip: Think of the apostrophe as a pointer, or an arrow, pointing to the *owner*, or to the *place* where something is omitted.

It's [shows where "i" goes]   Girl's, girls' [shows who owns]

1.1 Use the apostrophe to show possessive case (not always actual ownership).

Examples:

The boy's bicycle (The arrow/apostrophe points to *boy*, so we know that only one boy owns the bike.)

The boys' bicycle (It points to *boys*, so we know ownership is shared—it's owned by two or more boys.)

Where is the men's room?

Can you direct me to the Joneses' house?

Woman's room (It belongs to one woman.)

Women's room (Be careful here. Because *women* itself is plural, *womens'* would be an error, and so would *mens'.)*

Notes:

- With singular nouns ending in an *s*, *sh*, or *z* sound, use either an *apostrophe* and an *s*, or an *apostrophe* alone. Either is okay.

- The possessive case doesn't always mean real ownership. The "pointer" rule still applies, though: *a day's work, three hours' time, two weeks' wages.*

- When two co-owners are identified separately, you can show possession by the last-named owner or by both owners—your choice.

  Last-named owner: *Bill and Martha's kid*

  Both: *Bill's and Martha's kid*

- When the possessive case applies to each noun separately, each takes the possessive form.

  Bill's and Martha's cars (Each has separate ownership of at least one car.)

  Tom's and Jerry's school grades

- The apostrophe is usually added to the end of compound forms:
  my mother-in-law's car, the Queen of England's chauffeur.

1.2 Use the apostrophe in contractions, to show where something has been left out (usually by pointing to the place).

Examples:

  isn't, don't, the summer of '85, blizzard of '93

1.3 Use the apostrophe with some plurals.

Examples:

  *Dot your **i**'s and cross your **t**'s.*

  *Mind your **p**'s and **q**'s.*

  *Don't give me any **if**'s, **and**'s, or **but**'s.*

  *There are too many **&**'s and **#**'s on this page.*

  *She has two **Ph.D.**'s and three **M.A.**'s.*

Notes:

- DO NOT USE APOSTROPHES with possessive pronouns: *ours, yours, theirs, hers, its* (***it's*** means "it is" or sometimes "it has"), or *whose* (***who's*** means "who is" or sometimes "who has").

- Abbreviations that have periods inside and at the end usually take an apostrophe and an *s;* those with no periods (or with only final periods) take only the *s.*

  The school awarded 34 Ph.D.'s.

  Our group hired three MBAs last year.

- Names of organizations are often written without apostrophes — *Officers Club, Citizens Bank, Ladies Aid.* It's the organization's choice. So check it out, do it their way.

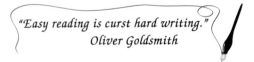

  "Easy reading is curst hard writing."
  Oliver Goldsmith

Semicolons

▣ 1.4 Use semicolons between independent clauses (ones that could stand alone as complete sentences) that are NOT joined by one of these words: *and, but, or, nor, for*—and sometimes *so, yet.* (These words are called "pure" or "coordinating" conjunctions.)

Hints:

- If you find yourself looking at two independent clauses, ask yourself if the clauses are joined by one of the pure conjunctions.
- If they are, use a comma.

  It's a challenging job, but I know you can do it.

  I won't run, for I hate politics.

  I understand the rule, and I'll use it.

- If they are not, use a semicolon.

  The previous quarter was a tough one; the next quarter may be even tougher.

  She planned to leave on Thursday; however, she could not get away until Saturday evening.

Note: Some good writers use a comma between short, contrasting independent clauses in sentences like this one:

  She left, he stayed behind.

▣ 1.5 Use semicolons to separate parts of a series when one part (or more) has internal commas.

Examples:

  We'll need paint, brushes, and thinner; nails, hammers, and a saw; and three good carpenters.

  He brought wine, soda, and glasses; and bread, cheese, and fruit.

Note: DO NOT USE SEMICOLONS to separate items just because they follow a colon.

  We chose Landa for three reasons: the quality of the training, the clarity of the examples, and the savoir-faire of the instructors.

  Not: *"…the quality of the training; the clarity of the examples…."*

Colons

Rule 1.6 Use a colon before a long or formal quotation or statement.

Example:

> *The senator rose, looked around, and began:*

Rule 1.7 Use a colon before a clarifying or illustrating item or series.

Examples:

> *Assembly will require three things: pliers, a screwdriver, and patience.*
>
> *We have only one thing to fear: fear itself.*
>
> *Mnemonics are like jokes: our own are always better.*

Rule 1.8 Use a colon after the salutation of a formal letter.

Example:

> *Dear Senator Lane:*

Rule 1.9 Use a colon between hours and minutes, chapter and verse.

Example:

> *10:46 p.m., John 3:16*

Quotation Marks

Rule 1.10 Use quotation marks to enclose someone else's exact words.

Examples:

> *"No," she said, "I'll never do that."*
>
> *"Frankly, my dear," he replied, "I'm careless."*

Notes:

- With a quotation of more than one paragraph, use quotation marks at the beginning of each paragraph, and at the end of the whole quotation.
- Long or formal quotations are sometimes centered (indented from both sides), with *no* quotation marks.

Rule 1.11 Use quotation marks to enclose parts (not wholes) of publications (see "Italics" at the end of this section for a broader listing).

Examples:

> One chapter of the book is called *"Way of the Wind."*
>
> *Time* has an article called *"Where Are the Flowers?"*
>
> *"The Raven" is in Collected Works of Poe.*
>
> We read the *"Style"* section of *The Washington Post.*

Rule 1.12 Use quotation marks to enclose words used in an unusual sense.

Example:

> *She used the paddle to "encourage" her students.*

Rule 1.13 Use quotation marks to enclose words, letters, numbers.

Example:

> *There are two "2's" and three "but's" in this sentence.* (These are sometimes underlined or italicized instead.)

Using Quotes With Other Marks:

Quotes used with other marks cause a lot of trouble. Here are the American rules (British rules are different).

- Periods and commas go **inside** the closing quotes. (Remember: they're small, so they slip inside easily.)

  She said "No," but later said "Maybe."

- Semicolons and colons (bigger) go **outside**.

  She said "Never"; I think that's her final answer.

- Question marks and exclamation marks go with the words that ask the question or show emotion.

  Did he say "Yes"?

  He said, "What have we here?"

  "Let's get out of here—this pressure gauge says '1800'!"

  The defendant then brandished a pistol and shouted "Holdup!"

- Use single quotes for a quote within a quote.

  He turned and said, "The admiral's reply was 'Nuts,' and that's my answer to you as well."

- Use brackets to insert your own words into quoted material.

  He said, "Whenever I see that car [the Reo], I smile."

  The exact words of the clerk were: "Whom [sic] shall I say is calling?"

  "Here are a couple of pounds for petrol [gasoline] for the trip," Sidney said.

Notes:

- DO NOT USE QUOTATION MARKS with **indirect** quotations.

  She said that she'll do it.

- DO NOT USE QUOTATION MARKS with well-known or humorous expressions.

  ***Not**: We must "put our shoulders to the wheel" to reach our goals.*

Periods

Rule 1.14 Use periods after declarative sentences (those that make statements).

Examples:

We learn many things in class.

Terminal punctuation is a dread disease.

Rule 1.15 Use periods after indirect questions that are phrased as declarative sentences.

Examples:

He wondered where she could be.

She asked where the zircon was.

***But**: Did she ask where the zircon was?*

"Our future depends on how well we inform each other —to fail in the use of language is clearly an unsocial act."

Robert Gunning, writing consultant

1.16 Use periods after polite requests phrased as questions.

Examples:

> *Will you please mail me a catalog.*
>
> *Waiter, may I have the check.*
>
> *Will you please come by to discuss your promotion.*
>
> *Can you come to the president's office one day this week.*
>
> *But: May I borrow your new car, Sid?*
>
> *Would you mind if I copied your paper?*
>
> *Can you tell me where the secret society meets?*

Note: A good test—ask yourself if a negative reply would be reasonable. If so, use a question mark; if not, use a period.

1.17 Use periods after directions or mild commands.

Examples:

> *Go to your separate meeting rooms now.*
>
> *Get out your exercise books.*
>
> *Report to the office right away.*

1.18 Use periods after most abbreviations (check your dictionary if you're not sure).

Examples:

> *Ph.D., Maj. Chris Smith, Ms. Johnson*
>
> *But: HUD, CIA, PX, etc.*

Note: If an abbreviation comes at the end of a sentence, use only one period.

> *Washington, D.C., is where we met.*
>
> *But: We met in Washington, D.C.*

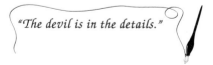

"The devil is in the details."

RULE 1.19 Use periods in threes (ellipsis) to show where something has been left out.

Examples:

"Give me liberty, or...death."

Add a fourth period if needed to end a sentence. "Give me liberty...."

Note: A typographical ellipsis character is available in most word-processing programs.

Question Marks

RULE 1.20 Use question marks after *direct* (not indirect) questions.

Examples:

What will you have?

***But:** He asked what you'll have.* ***Not:** ...what you'll have?*

RULE 1.21 Use questions marks to indicate the writer's uncertainty.

Example:

Shakespeare's birth (on April 23?) was an important event.

RULE 1.22 Use question marks after each "little question" in an unlettered, unnumbered series within a sentence.

Examples:

Did you ask about his family? his profession? his income?

Do we have sugar? flour? butter?

Exclamation Points

RULE 1.23 Use an exclamation point after a forceful interjection, to show strong feelings.

RULE 1.24 Use exclamation points rarely.

Note: Overuse of the exclamation point is considered a sign of immature writing. This mark is rarely used in business correspondence or in other formal writing.

Commas

Rule 1.25 Use a comma to separate independent clauses joined by a coordinating (pure) conjunction: *and, but, or, nor, for* (and sometimes *so, yet*).

Examples:

> *We waited all night, but the plane didn't arrive.*
>
> *The office picnic was great, and the food was excellent.*

Rule 1.26 Use a comma to set off *introductory* words, clauses, and phrases.

Examples:

> *After lunch, we had dessert.*
>
> *When he read the report, he was startled.*
>
> ***But:*** *He was startled when he read the report.*

Rule 1.27 Use commas to set off "nonessential" sentence elements.

Note:

- In the first sentence below, *who works hard* is not essential to identifying the person who will succeed. In the second, *who works hard* is essential.

> *Margaret, who works hard, will succeed.*
>
> *A person who works hard will succeed.*

Examples:

> *The supervisor, a volatile man, began shouting.*
>
> *The poet Dickenson is a superb wordsmith.*

Rule 1.28 Use commas to separate items in a series.

Example:

> *We had tea, toast, and marmalade. (The last comma is optional.)*

> *"...use of the comma is mainly a matter of good judgment, with ease of reading as the end in view."*
> *Chicago Manual of Style*

⊞ 1.29 Use commas to separate *coordinate* (equal) adjectives.

Notes:

- To test for comma use, ask yourself if the word *"and"* could go between the adjectives without changing the meaning. If so, use a comma.

  She was a thoughtful, attentive, careful writer.

  The old, ragged, mud-stained coat was discovered.

- If the word *"and"* does not seem okay, don't use a comma.

  We're planning an exciting Christmas swim party.

⊞ 1.30 Use commas to set off the main elements in dates or places.

Examples:

  May 3, 2000 (But: May 2000, spring 2001)

  He lived at 10 Main St., Erwin, Tennessee.

⊞ 1.31 Use commas to prevent misreading.

Examples:

  Long before, he had written his will.

  Still, water is needed on the farm.

⊞ 1.32 Use commas to set off nouns of direct address.

Examples:

  Yes, Nate, you must rewrite this.

  Sir, you may come in now.

  You're wonderful, teacher.

⊞ 1.33 Use commas to set off direct quotations (someone's exact words).

Example:

  "No," she said, "it was Randolph."

⊞ 1.34 Use commas with inverted names.

Example:

  Smith, Edward

Rule 1.35 Use a comma after the salutation of a personal letter.

Example:

Dear John,

Rule 1.36 Use commas to separate (into groups of three) numbers of five or more digits.

Example:

186,300 mps

Notes:

- DO NOT USE A COMMA between subject and verb.

  Not: The ruler of the island chain, was a huge woman.

- DO NOT USE A COMMA after the last item of a series.

  Not: We had soda, cheese, and crackers, before dinner.

Parentheses

Note: Use parentheses in pairs (one is a parenthesis).

Rule 1.37 Use parentheses to set off something added to clarify, explain, etc.

Examples:

You'll need a pop-rivet gun (from a hardware store) and a file.

He spoke often of Guam (he'd spent a year there) and of Irma (his former nurse).

Note: In technical directions, brackets are often used.

Attach the gimflay [item 9] to the main fribble bar.

Rule 1.38 Use parentheses to set off numbers or letters used as list-indicators.

Example:

The area produces (1) tobacco, (2) corn, and (3) dairy products.

"In all cases, the use of rules should be balanced with good judgment."
Dictionary editor

Brackets

Rule 1.39 Use brackets to set off something inserted into quoted material.

Examples:

> *The reviewer wrote, "This actor [Connor O'Brien] is great."*
>
> *He picked up the phone and said, "Whom [sic] shall I say is calling?"*

Rule 1.40 Use brackets as parentheses within parentheses.

Example:

> *They invited one politician (Senator Kennedy [D-Mass.]) and one businessman.*

Rule 1.41 Use brackets to clarify directions.

Examples:

> *Buy the gasket [available at auto-supply stores], and carefully study the diagram [Fig. 3-A] before you install it.*

Hyphens

Rule 1.42 Use a hyphen to divide a word at the end of a line.

Rule 1.43 Use hyphens with unit modifiers (especially if needed to clarify).

Examples:

> *a little-read book*
> *a small-dog show*
> *a foreign-trade advocate*
> *a long-forgotten letter*

> *"If you take hyphens seriously you will surely go mad."*
> *John Benbow,*
> *in the Oxford University Press Stylebook*

▨ 1.44 Use hyphens with some compounds.

Note: All spelled-out, two-word numbers from twenty-one through ninety-nine are hyphenated; so are "self" compounds.

"self" compounds: *self-destructive, self-starting*

compound numbers: *twenty-one, ninety-nine*

▨ 1.45 Use hyphens to avoid tripling a consonant: *cell-like.*

▨ 1.46 Use a hyphen to prevent confusion with another word.

Examples:

re-form (to shape again)
re-creation (to make again)
re-petition (to ask again)
re-present (to give again)
re-lease (to rent again)

Dashes

Note: Dashes are sometimes written as two hyphens; however, most word-processing software provides a dash character, called an "em dash." (A shorter dash, called the "en dash," is also available.)

▨ 1.47 Use em dashes to show a sudden change or break in a sentence.

Example:

They elected—can you believe this?—Melvyn Dorquey.

▨ 1.48 Use em dashes before words that summarize.

Example:

Sailing, singing, and sunning ourselves—those were our only tasks.

▨ 1.49 You may use en dashes instead of hyphens to show inclusive numbers.

Examples:

June 4–6, 1987; pages 432–485; 4:00 p.m.–6:00 p.m.

Interrupters

Punctuation marks (usually commas, parentheses, or dashes) are used to set off something inserted into a sentence.

Hints:

- For normal breaks, use commas.

  The pitcher, Johnson, was hurt.

- For slightly stronger breaks, use parentheses.

  The coat (an old, tattered thing) lay on the chair.

- For even stronger breaks, use dashes.

  That man—I'll never know where he came from—saved our lives.

Italics

Note: If you are writing by hand or using a typewriter, <u>underline</u> where italics would be used. (E.g., I'm reading <u>War and Peace</u>.)

1.50 Use italics to emphasize words (use sparingly).

1.51 Use italics to mark foreign terms.

Example:

C'est la vie means "that's life."

1.52 Use italics with certain titles (e.g., book titles).

Note: It's hard to remember whether to use italic type or quotation marks for different kinds of titles. A good rule is to use italics for titles of *whole* works, and quotes for titles of *parts* or *sections* (or short works). This chart gives more detail:

Use Italics (or underlining)	Use Quotes
Books (except sacred works like Bible, Koran, Torah)	Chapters
	Essays
Magazines	Articles
Newspapers	Stories, columns
Movies	Speeches
Plays	Radio or TV programs
Art works	Songs, poems
Craft (ships, trains, planes, spacecraft)	

2 Numbers

Section

Note: These rules about numbers are useful guides, but many professional writers and editors sometimes ignore them.

Rule 2.1 Write out numbers one through nine; use numerals for 10 and higher.

Examples:

> *The awards go to six of our students.*
>
> *She read 18 books last term.*

Notes and exceptions:

- This "nine and under" rule applies especially to correspondence (like memos and letters).
- For longer works (e.g., complete books), many editors spell out numbers one through ninety-nine, and use numerals for 100 and higher.
- Use hyphens in compound numbers.

  twenty-four, one hundred thirty-six, nineteen fifty-two, two-thirds

Rule 2.2 Spell out a number at the beginning of a sentence.

Example:

> *Five hundred people attended the event.*

Rule 2.3 Numerals are usually used for dates, time of day, house numbers, page numbers, percentages, decimals, degrees, money, etc.

Examples:

> *6 May 1991, 9:30 a.m., 10 Elm Street, page 4, 14%, 3.1416, 90°, $2.98*

Rule 2.4 Numbers like *first, second, third* (called "ordinal numbers" because they show order) are usually spelled out through *ninth*, and written as numerals (10th, 21st) beyond that.

Examples:

> *the fifth column, the 17th century, 11th Street, the third verse*

Section 3 Capital Letters

Here are some of the most-helpful rules. Use a good dictionary or style manual for questions not covered here.

Rule 3.1 Capitalize proper nouns (the names of *specific* persons, places, or things); DO NOT capitalize common nouns.

Examples:

The general	*General Westly*
Our doctor	*Our physician, Dr. Johnson*
His division	*The Blivit Division*
The club president	*The President of France*

Rule 3.2 Capitalize recognized geographical sections; DO NOT capitalize compass directions.

Examples:

He's from the South.	*We drove south.*

Rule 3.3 Don't capitalize the seasons: *next spring, last summer.*

Rule 3.4 Don't capitalize family-relationship terms except when used as names.

Examples:

My father knew best.	*May I, Mother?*
I respected my aunt.	*Hello, Aunt Fannie.*

Rule 3.5 Capitalize the first word and other important words in titles of publications, poems, art works, etc.

Examples:

The Day of the Locust	"In a Boat with a Pony"

Section 4 Grammar

Parts of Speech

Noun

Names a person, place, or thing.
Chris *is a good* **student**.

Pronoun

Stands for a noun (its *antecedent*).
The **man** (noun, antecedent) *called* **his** (pronoun) *dog*.
A pronoun should agree with its antecedent in person, number, and gender.

Verb

Shows action, condition, or being.
Verbs **are** *important*.
A verb should agree with its subject in number.

Adjective

Modifies (tells about) a noun or pronoun.
Good *writers deserve* **high** *praise*.

Adverb

Modifies a verb, adjective, or adverb.
They don't **always** *get it*.

Conjunction

Joins words and word-groups.
Grammar **and** *punctuation*....

Preposition

Relates a noun or pronoun (the object) to another word.
We're looking **into** *it*.

Interjection

A word "thrown into" the sentence.
Wow! *This is a great little book.*

Parts of Sentence

Verb Shows action, condition, being.
I **love** *grammar.*

Subject Shows who/what is acting, being.
I *love grammar.*

Direct Object Receives the action of the verb.
She wrote him a **memo.**

Indirect Object Shows to or for whom something is done.
She wrote **him** *a memo.*

Predicate Completes predicate (verb), "renames" subject.
Nominative *Lee is the* **deputy.**

Predicate Completes predicate (verb), modifies subject.
Adjective *Lee is* **intelligent.**

Appositive Follows and "renames" a noun or pronoun.
Lee, the **deputy,** *is intelligent.*

Modifier A word, phrase, or clause that modifies another part of the
sentence. (Adjectives and adverbs are modifiers.)
Give the book to the **tall** *woman* **in red.**
The sentry **who guards the gate** *was alert.*

Interjection A word thrown into the sentence.
Great, *you aced the test.*

Verbals

Note: Verbals are hybrids—part verb, part something else.

Gerund A verbal noun (part verb, part noun).
Sailing *can be relaxing or exciting.*
We enjoyed John's **singing.**

Participle A verbal adjective.
Sailing can be **relaxing** *or* **exciting.**
The **burnt** *toast was discarded.*
The **revised** *memo was signed.*

Infinitive	A verbal noun, adjective, or adverb.
	To hesitate *is* **to lose**. (noun)
	The horse **to watch** *is Fury*. (adjective)
	He plays **to win**. (adverb)

Note: It's okay to split an infinitive, as in *to really try, to closely watch, to gladly learn*.

Agreement: Subject and Verb

Rules are intended to be helpful, but they can get us in trouble if we trust them too much. The one on subject-verb agreement can be a little dangerous. Here's the rule:

⊞4.1 The verb agrees with its subject in number: both should be singular, or both plural.

Discussion:

Most of the sentences that give us problems in subject/verb agreement have something between the subject and verb. If we're not careful, we'll make the verb agree with that something, instead of with the subject. Look at these sentences.

The singer, along with seven of her associates, is scheduled to perform next week.

The camshaft, as well as two of the linking pins and five bolts, was badly corroded.

To fight and to win is our aim.

To apply the rule, look first for the verb, then look carefully for the subject of that verb. That should give us *singer* and *camshaft* as the subjects of the first two examples, so we use singular verbs. No problem.

But the third example has *two* subjects—"to fight" and "to win"—so we need the plural form of the verb: "are." But that would look funny, correct or not. And according to that rule, these next sentences are also correct:

The greatest fear of the natives is two wild animals.

Three fine singers are the trio we've booked.

And sentences like these—or worse—have been printed in good, respected publications. They are "correct," but they look funny, and they sound funny. If you find that you've written a sentence like that, don't worry about whether the rule says it's okay—just go ahead and rewrite. (E.g., We've booked a trio of three fine singers.) Make sure your revision is correct, but also make sure your readers won't stub their eyes over it.

Active and Passive Sentences

What Is an Active Sentence?

To many people, an active sentence is simply one that shows some kind of action, and a passive sentence is one that doesn't. So those people would say that "The car was blown to pieces" is an active sentence, and that "The committee considered several alternatives" is a passive sentence.

But to most English teachers, writers, and editors, it's the other way around. An active (or *active-voice*) sentence is one in which the *subject does something to an object*. So "She diagrammed the sentence" and "The committee considered alternatives" are both active sentences.

In a passive (or *passive-voice*) sentence, the *subject receives the action*. "The car was blown to pieces" is passive, and so is "The hyena was crushed by the elephant."

Are Active Sentences Always Better than Passive Ones?

No, they aren't. The truth is that the passive voice can be stronger than the active. Take this sentence: "The President has been shot." It's a clear, strong sentence, even though it's passive.

Now how about this one: "Someone named John Hinckley has shot the President." It's sure enough active—the subject acts on an object. But it's weaker than the first one, because the subject is not the important element here. By including an unknown (at the time) doer, the writer distracts the reader from the important stuff.

So why do passive sentences have a bad reputation? One reason is that some writers do hide behind the passive, using it as a screen to hide their identities. Examples:

> *Your request has been denied.*
>
> *Your loan application is hereby disapproved.*
>
> *Your policy has been canceled.*
>
> *A serious mistake has been made.*

Who's invisible in these sentences? The doer, that's who. The reader is being done unto, but doesn't know who's doing it.

Write Clear, Strong Sentences.

We recommend (notice the active voice) that you work hard to write clear, strong sentences, rather than trying too hard to identify and eliminate the passive voice. You'll automatically end up with fewer passive sentences—and they'll be good ones.

Is every sentence either active or passive? No. Only *transitive* sentences (those in which some action goes *across* the verb, either to or from the subject) are classified as active or passive. When no action is exchanged from doer to receiver, the sentence is *intransitive*. (Transitive sentences: *Birds catch flies. Curiosity killed the cat.* Intransitive sentences: *Birds fly. Carelessness kills.*)

Agreement: Pronoun and Antecedent

Note: A pronoun is a word that takes the place of a noun (the antecedent).

⊞ 4.2 The pronoun should agree with its antecedent in number, person, and gender.

Notes:

- There are four genders in English: Masculine, feminine, common, and neuter (*John/he, Anne/she, people/they, table/it*).
- There are two "numbers": Singular and plural (*child, children*).
- There are three "persons": First (person speaking: *I*), second (person spoken to: *you*), and third (person/thing spoken of: *he/she/it*).

Discussion:

One big problem with our language is that English has no singular possessive pronoun that applies to both males and females (common gender). We have to use either the masculine or feminine, so we wind up writing gems like these:

Each executive must budget his time.

Anyone who asks can get their money back.

The first example has a masculine pronoun (his), and the writer could be accused of sexism. The second example has a disagreement in number (anyone-their). How to fix? "His/her" is awkward, as is "his or her." Why not change the pronouns and their antecedents to the plural forms?

"Executives...their time."

"Customers...their money...."

"I can't understand how anyone can write without rewriting over and over again."
Leo Tolstoy

David Hatcher and Lane Goddard

Case: "Just Between You and I"

Everybody has trouble with grammar rules sometimes. Although they may not like to admit it, even English teachers and professional writers and editors get tangled up in their words now and then.

One common problem is the use of the wrong pronoun form (or case). Standard English requires the *subjective* case (also called *nominative* case) for the subject of the sentence. (Examples of subjective-case pronouns are *I, we, he, she.*)

And the *objective* case is used for the direct object, object of the preposition, etc. (Objective-case pronouns include *me, us, him,* and *her.*) Look at these examples:

> They invited Chris and I to attend the conference.
>
> If they're free, I'll ask Charlie and he to join us.
>
> Just between you and I, the project is way behind schedule.

Cause and Cure

First, what's wrong with the sentences? The answer is that each uses a subjective-case pronoun where the objective case is needed.

Second, how can we avoid or correct such sentences? There's some good news here, because we don't have to learn a lot of complicated rules. In almost all such sentences, a big part of the problem is that there are two words (usually connected by *and*) used as the same part of the sentence. If we simply *leave out the other word for a moment*, we'll see the problem.

In the first example, let's leave Chris out. That gives us: *They invited I to attend the conference.* It's instantly clear that we need to use *me* instead of *I.*

In the second example, setting the other word aside leaves us asking *he* to join us. No problem, we'll change it to *him.*

The third is just a little harder, because we wouldn't say *between I.* But once you've got the principle, you can see that it should read *between you and me.*

Summary

In most of our problems with case, there's a second word that confuses us. So when in doubt, leave it out—long enough to see which form of the pronoun to use, then put it back in.

"If a reader can't understand my writing, he's just dumb."

A Dumb Writer

To Whom, or Not To Whom

If you use *whom*, some people will think you're pretentious. But if you don't, others will think your language is too plain. And if you *misuse* it, you're in double-trouble (for trying, and for failing).

So when should you use *whom* (instead of *who*)? Here are two answers—a long one, and a short one.

The Long Answer

The longer one first. Whenever you're trying to decide whether to use *who* or *whom*, first find every verb in the sentence, then find the *subject* of each verb. Use *who* (or *whoever*) as the subject. Use *whom* (or *whomever*) as the object.

To see how this works, look at this sentence from a major newspaper:

> *The actress, whom the tabloids say is very ill, was flown from California to her home in Switzerland.*

There are three verbs in the sentence: ***say***, ***is***, and ***was flown***. To find the subject of the first, ask "Who says?" The answer gives you the subject: **the tabloids**. Repeat with the other verbs, and you get ***the actress*** was flown, and ***whom*** is ill. Aha—they goofed. Because it's the subject of the verb "is," the *who* form is required.

That's a pretty complicated sentence, the kind that causes trouble for even professionals (like the people who wrote, edited, and proofread it). It sort of sounds like it should be *whom*, doesn't it? And that's why so many good writers misuse it, and why we need to follow this verb-subject process if we're going to avoid *who/whom* errors.

The Short Answer

Now for the short answer. Don't use *whom*. It doesn't add much to your writing, and it can get you into trouble. Try to write around it—change the sentence. Use *whom/whomever* only when you have to (which is almost never).

Note: Although it rarely comes up, you should remember that the *who* form is also used as the predicate nominative, as in "*It was who?*"

More Examples

Look at this sentence:

> *He criticizes* **whom***?*

The sentence is okay. *Whom* is the direct object—it receives the action of the verb *criticizes*. We get used to sentences like that, and then we run into one like this:

> *"He criticizes* **whomever** *makes a mistake."*

It looks okay at first glance, because it starts just like the one before it. It sort of *feels* like a sentence with a direct object, so the writer used the object form: *whomever*.

But it's a tricky sentence—the kind that'll bite us. The sentence *does* have a direct object, but it's not *whom*. The direct object is a whole clause.

A clause is a group of words with a subject and a verb. The verb is *makes,* so what is the *subject* of that verb? You ask "Who makes?" The answer is *whomever.* So the clause has a grammatical error—it uses an object form (whomever) as a subject. To correct it, you change the pronoun to *whoever.* (Or even better, revise it—to something like "He criticizes anyone who makes a mistake.")

"The most loathsome word...in the English language is whom."
        Kyle Crichton, Associate Editor, Collier's

The Subjunctive

What Is the Subjunctive Mood?

Moods (sometimes called *modes*) are verb forms we use to tell readers and listeners what we're doing with our sentences—stating a fact, giving an order, or talking about something we know *not* to be true. There are three moods, and only one causes trouble.

- **The indicative mood**, by far the most common, is used for ordinary statements and questions. *We're studying grammar, Isn't this fun,* etc.

- **The imperative mood** is used for strong commands and orders (it often takes an exclamation point). *Go! Desist!*

- **The subjunctive mood** is used to show serious doubt, wish or probability, and condition *contrary to fact.*

How Does This Affect You?

There are lots of rules about the subjunctive, but the one that follows is probably more important than all the others combined, because it's the one that you're most likely to need in your writing and editing.

⊞4.3 In your formal or work-related writing, use *were* instead of *was* in *contrary-to-fact clauses* like the ones below.

Examples:

If I were an executive, I wouldn't have to study grammar.

I wish it weren't so cloudy out today.

Were I not so busy, I'd do it myself.

If Martin were alive today, he'd be proud of you.

He talks as if he were eating mush.

If Walt were here, he'd know what to do.

Notes:

- **Good tip:** Use the "but-not" test to help when you're in doubt. In the first example above, you'd say "If I was/were an executive..." *but I'm not.* Because the speaker is not an executive, we have what the grammarians call a "condition contrary to fact," so we'd use the subjunctive form *were.*

- **Careful:** Sometimes you'll find a clause or sentence that *looks like* it might be subjunctive, but leaves us in doubt. The but-not test can help, because if something *is probably true*, or *might well have been* true, you *would not* use the subjunctive. As an example, suppose your mail carrier *always* comes before noon, and *usually* leaves mail for you. You check at mid-afternoon, and find your mailbox empty. Because the mail carrier *probably had* been by, you would not use the subjunctive *were*. Instead, you'd use the plain old indicative *was*: "If the mail carrier was here, he didn't leave anything." Similar examples:

If Chris was the winner, she didn't brag about it.

I believe Kim was the captain, but I'm not sure.

If I was alone with her, I don't remember it.

Here are two sentences that may help show when to use the indicative, and when to use the subjunctive:

If the janitor was here [and he may well have been], he didn't fix the leak.

If the janitor were here [but he isn't], he'd know how to fix the leak.

A Final Word

For more than a hundred years, scholars have been saying that the subjunctive is disappearing. It's not used nearly as much as it was in the past, but it's still here, and it's still complicated. Professional writers, editors, and teachers have trouble deciding when to use it, so don't feel bad if you're not always sure about it. When in doubt, try to revise the sentence—write your way around the problem.

The subjunctive is disappearing from our language, and will soon be gone.

Dictionary editor, ca 1877

Section 5 Spelling

Rule 5.1 "It's easier to learn to spell than to learn the spelling rules."

Frustrated student

Discussion:

English spelling is inconsistent, nonphonetic, and sometimes downright weird. And some spelling rules are worse than a waste of time, because they're more likely to get you into trouble than to help you.

What's the most common spelling rule? "*I* before *e* except after *c*, or when sounded like *a* as in **neighbor** or **weigh**."

Many books include that rule. One recent and respected grammar book includes it, but points out that there are five exceptions. Another book lists eight exceptions, a third gives nine.

Without much effort (and with no computer help), we've come up with more than 50 exceptions. And people who learn the rule (and eight or nine exceptions) are less likely to look up ie/ei words they're not sure about—so they're more likely to misspell the other exceptions.

But not all rules are bad. Here are some that can be helpful.

Rule 5.2 Drop a final *e* before adding *ing*.

Examples:

Joke	Joking
Drape	Draping
Force	Forcing
Write	Writing

- Exceptions include *dyeing, shoeing, hoeing,* and many others.

5.3 Double a final consonant if its syllable is accented.

Examples:

Conferred	*Conferring*	*Conference*
Preferred	*Preferring*	*Preference*
Redder	*Redden*	
Forbidden	*Forbidding*	

5.4 Change *y* to *i* before adding *ed* and most other suffixes, but not before adding *ing*.

Examples:

Ladies	*Tried*	*Trying*
Sullied	*Cried*	*Crying*

Note: Attorney, attorneys (not *attornies*)

5.5 Pluralize the main word in most compounds.

Examples:

Mothers-in-law	*Courts-martial*
Commanders in chief	*Ladies-in-waiting*

5.6 Keep an e after "S-sounding" C and after "J-sounding" G.

Examples:

Peaceable	*Serviceable*
Courageous	*Changeable*

The preceding rules can be helpful, but they won't get rid of our spelling problems. We'll do better if we admit that we're not perfect, and use the following spelling rules to help reduce the number of misspelled words that sneak into our writing.

"You write a swell letter. Glad somebody spells worse than I do."
Ernest Hemingway
to F. Scott Fitzgerald

Spelling Rules That Work

- Use your spellchecker, but *don't* depend on it entirely.

- Keep a good dictionary in reach, and reach for it often.

- Ask someone who's a good speller to proofread your work.

- Learn or make up memory aids: (There's *a rat* in *separate*.)

- Keep your own list of troublesome words. Use the list.

My Own Spelling List

You'll benefit greatly if you keep a list of words *you* have trouble with, and think up a memory aid for each (the capit**O**l is a d**O**med building). Add other words to your list, keep it handy, and use it (maybe in friendly spelling contests with others who want to improve).

Spelling: One Hundred Hard Ones

These words are not the most difficult ones to spell. Words like *syzygy* and *sphygmomanometer* are tougher—but we hardly ever use them. We use the words below a lot, and they cause about 95% of our everyday spelling problems. So this list can help you make a big improvement in your spelling, with a small investment of time and effort.

absence	discriminate	principal*
accessible	dissension	privilege
accessory	dissipate	procedure
accommodate	embarrass	proceed
achieve	exceed	professor
all right	existence	pronunciation
allotted	forty	pursue
already	grammar	realtor
analyze	harass	receive
argument	holiday	recommend
assistant	incidentally	repetition
attorneys	indispensable	ridiculous
balloon	inoculate	role
benefited	insistent	seize
calendar	irritable	separate
capitol*	leisure	sergeant
category	liaison	sheriff
changeable	license	sole
committee	maintenance	stationery*
comparative	misspell	succeed
complement*	necessary	superintendent
conscience	nickel	supersede*
conscious	noticeable	surprise
corroborate	nuclear	tariff
consensus	occasion	truly
definitely	occurrence	until (but *till*)
description	parallel	vacillate
desert*	paralyze	vacuum
desirable	perseverance	vicious
despair	persistent	waive
development	possess	weird
dilemma	precede	you're*
disappear	predictable	
disappoint	prerogative	

See Section 8, "Confusable Words."

Section 6 Language & Gender

Webster's New World Dictionary defines sexism as discrimination against people on the basis of sex (specifically, discrimination against women). Sexist language presents an unfair picture of a group of people on the basis of their gender.

We know that prejudice can have many objects. People can be discriminated against because of race, appearance, speech patterns, the way they dress, the places they come from, and for many other reasons—including the way they write.

They can also be discriminated against because of their gender, and that's why sexist language is a concern to us.

One common form of sexist language reflects stereotypical images of females (e.g., as people who are helpless in dealing with anything mechanical). We don't see much of this language anymore, but the more subtle forms are still very much with us—and more difficult to detect and avoid.

And even less common—but every bit as unfair—are sexist references to males. This may be a backlash, or an attempt to get even with antifeminist men. Whatever the reason, sexist language should be avoided.

Nobody can provide a foolproof formula for keeping sexism out of your language, but the following rules will help.

Rule 6.1 Don't use single-sex pronouns (like *he, she, his, hers, him, her*) when referring to both sexes.

Examples:

>*Instead of*: Each executive must fill out his weekly expense voucher.
>*Say*: Each executive must fill out a weekly expense voucher.
>*Or*: All executives must fill out weekly expense vouchers.

6.2 Be careful with single-sex pronouns for professions and careers.

Examples:

> *Instead of*: You should see a doctor and get his advice.
> *Say*: You should get a doctor's advice.

> *Instead of*: A good nurse is well worth her pay.
> *Say*: Good nurses are well worth what they're paid.

6.3 Use "girl" and "boy" only when referring to children.

Examples:

> *Instead of*: I'll have my girl call your girl for an appointment.
> *Say*: I'll ask my secretary to call and set up an appointment.

> *Instead of*: Can you send a few of your boys to help?
> *Say*: Can you send a few people over to help out?

6.4 Be consistent in the use of titles.

Examples:

> *Instead of*: Ask Barbara and Mr. Smith to attend.
> *Say*: Ask Ms. Jones and Mr. Smith to attend.
> *Or*: Ask Barbara and Larry to attend.

6.5 Be consistent in any comments on physical appearance or professional competence.

Examples:

> *Don't say*: I work with some great-looking women and hard-working men.
> *Instead say*: The people I work with look and act like professionals.

6.6 Avoid overuse of "man" and "mankind."

Examples:

> *Instead of*: Freedom is the right of every man.
> *Say*: Freedom is the right of every person.

> *Instead of*: This is a benefit to mankind.
> *Say*: This is a benefit to humanity (or the world).

Section 7 Proofreading

Proofreader's Marks

Proofreader's marks are instructions—shorthand messages from the proofreader or editor to the person who keys in the changes. The marks must be clearly made, and everyone involved in the process must know what each mark means.

Not all publishers use the same marks, and some style books show many more than the ones below. But these are in common use, and should be all you need. If you do need more or different marks for the work you do, that's okay. Just be sure all the people working together understand what each mark means.

Mark	Meaning	Example
─●	Delete	We meet last night.
∧	Insert	We'll met later today.
∼	Transpose	We met lats night.
⌒	Close up	We met last ni ght.
#	Space	We met lastnight.
◯	Spell out	We stayed 5 days.
◯	Shorten	Doctor Lee stayed eleven days.
≡	Cap letter	i met john last night.
/	Small letter	I met John Last night.
⊙	Insert period	I met her last night⊙
⌐	Move left	I met her last night.
⌐	Move right	I met her last night.
⁋	Paragraph	So we left Spain. In Italy, we…
stet	Let stand	He had had two already.
───	Use italics	I'm reading Rabbit Run.

The Double-Bubble Method

Proofreader's marks can be effective time-savers when you're working with people who also know what the marks mean and how to use them. But if you're working with people who are unfamiliar with them, the marks can be confusing. So instead of using proofer's marks, you can use the "double-bubble" method of marking changes.

There are three simple steps in this method.

- Circle anything you want changed.

- Write in the margin clear instructions for making the change.

- Circle your instructions, and draw a line connecting the two circles (the bubbles).

Here's an example of the double-bubble method.

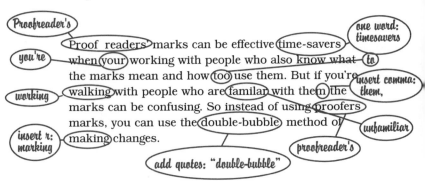

The double-bubble method may take more space and time, but it clearly shows what changes you want made. Many editors and proofreaders use some double-bubbles, along with standard marks.

Proofreading Hints

- You can't see your own mistakes, so have someone else proof your writing.
- Age the copy before rereading (if possible, let it sit overnight).
- Be a mean reader—be critical.
- Use a clean sheet of paper to cover the page below the line you're reading.
- Circle your proofing marks.
- Put tick-marks in the margins beside lines with changes.
- Agree on what marks to use, what they mean, and who makes final decisions.
- Read aloud to someone else (especially on lists, and on columns of numbers).
- Revise a "correct" sentence that doesn't sound right or that might offend your reader.

8 Confusable Words

Section 8

Be careful with these word-pairs—they cause lots of trouble, even for good writers.

Adopt/Adapt— To ad**o**pt is to voluntarily take as one's **O**wn: "Let's adopt this Latin phrase as our motto." To ad**a**pt is to ch**A**nge to suit conditions: "I didn't like the city at first, but I adapted."

Averse/Adverse— People are **averse**; conditions are **adverse**. "I'm not averse to an Alaskan vacation, but we may find adverse weather conditions there."

Among/Between— **Among** refers to three or more: "We had seven dollars among the three of us." **Between** usually refers to only two people or things: "Just between you and me...."

Affect/Effect— **Affect** as a verb means to change, influence: "His speech affected the election." **Effect** means to make happen: "It effected a victory for his party." Noun forms are explained below.

	Affect	**Effect**
As Nouns	*Affect* is very rarely used as a noun. (In psychology, it means roughly "emotional response.")	The **effect** is the **r**esult. *What will be the effect?*
As Verbs	Affect begins with an "A," means "change or sway." *Will the oil spill affect the water? Will the speech affect the vote?*	Effect begins with an "E," means "to cause it to be." *The new manager effected a reorganization of the division.*

Apprise/Appraise— To appr**i**se is to **i**nform: "Please keep me apprised of the patient's condition." To appr**a**ise is to **ra**te or evaluate: "I'm having my house appraised."

Bimonthly— Don't use **bimonthly**, because it is commonly used (and defined in good dictionaries) to mean both "twice a month" and "every two months."

Capitol/Capital— Remember that the domed building, the **capitol**, looks like an "O" from the air, and is spelled with one. The other "capitals" are spelled with an "A": the city, money, wealth, something excellent (a capital idea), letters, etc.

Compliment/Complement— Think "I like compliments," which are expressions of praise. A complement is something that completes, as in "That scarf is the perfect complement to your outfit." It's also the authorized size of staff, as in "The complement of the squadron is 12 enlisted personnel and one officer."

Compulsion/Compunction— **Compulsion** is that which compels. "She felt a compulsion to shoplift, even though she had plenty of money." **Compunction** is that little pinprick (as in puncture) of conscience about some thought or action, often noted for its absence. "He felt no compunction about giving the police the names of the drug dealers."

Counsel/Council— To **counsel** means to give advice (and counsel may also refer to the advisor, especially a lawyer); a **council** is a committee or group established for a specific purpose.

Criteria/Criterion— **Criteria** is plural; the singular is **criterion**.

Emigrate/Immigrate— To **emigrate** means to leave (**e**xit, **e**migrate); to **immigrate** means to come into (**i**n, **i**mmigrate), especially when referring to a permanent move to another country.

Eminent/Imminent— Some**one** who is outstanding (especially in a profession or respected field of work) is **eminent**. Some**thing** which appears likely to happen right away is **imminent**. **He** or **she** is **e**minent; **it** is **i**mminent.

Farther/Further— **Farther** refers to physical distance. **Further**, the purists say, means to a greater degree or extent, and shouldn't be used for physical distance. But *Webster's New World Dictionary* lists each as a synonym of the other. Recommendation: Use **farther** for physical distance, **further** for nonphysical uses. Don't try to convert others.

Flaunt/Flout— To **flaunt** is to make a display of (often a vulgar or ostentatious display); to **flout** is to brazenly disregard (as by smoking under a big "No Smoking" sign). However, *Webster's New World Dictionary* lists "flout" as one definition of "flaunt," adding that some object to this usage. It does not list the reverse—**flout** means only to scoff at, not to display.
Recommendation: Go with the purists; keep them separate.

Forego/Forgo— **Forego** means to go before; **forgo** means to go without. *Webster's New World Dictionary* lists **forego** as a variant spelling of **forgo**, but not the other way around. Keep them separate, but don't argue with those who use the one with the "e" for both meanings.

i.e./e.g.— These shouldn't be interchanged. To remember the difference, think of **i.e.** as an abbreviation for "it equals" (not too far from "that is," which the Latin *id est* means). This abbreviation is **not** used when giving an example, but when restating or defining to clarify, as in "He gave the correct password (i.e., *omfuddery*)." And **e.g.** (which means *exempli gratia*, or "for example") is the one you'll use when you want to give an example, or two or three, as in "They served dozens of odd dishes (e.g., rattlesnake and chocolate-covered ants)."

Imply/Infer— **Imply** means to hint or suggest something without saying it outright; **infer** means to understand what was hinted at, to read between the lines. Remember that the senders of messages (writers and speakers) imply. The receivers of messages (readers and listeners) infer. Use the middle letter of each as a clue—to imply is to **p**ut meaning in, and to in**f**er is to get meaning **f**rom the hints. (Some people use *infer* to mean "hint at," but that's often considered nonstandard.)

Ingenious/Ingenuous— An **ingenious** (in GENE yuss) person or idea is clever, intelligent, original. But **ingenuous** (in GIN you us) means simple, naive, incapable of dishonesty.

Its/It's— **Its** refers to something that belongs to (or is closely associated with) "it," as in "The dog wagged its tail, the bank closed its doors, the horse lost its shoe." **It's** means "it is" (or sometimes "it has"), as in "It's hot in here, it's too late for me to learn all these words, it's been a tough day."

Kudos/Kudo— **Kudos** is singular, meaning "praise," "glory," or "fame." There is no "kudo."

Lectern/Podium— The stand that holds the speaker's notes is a **lectern** (from the Latin *lectus*, "to read"). The raised platform at the front of a hall is a **podium**. (*Pod* comes from the Greek root for *foot*, as in tripod, biped, and pedestal.) But note that some dictionaries list "lectern" as one definition of podium.

Less/Fewer— **Less** is used for something in a mass—powder, air, and so on. **Fewer** is used for things that come in separate units, things you could count. So we put less salt in the soup, but fewer plates on the table. We may make less money, but we have fewer coins. (Note: Many people interchange these words freely.)

Militate/Mitigate— To **militate** against something is to make it less likely to happen: "His driving record will militate against his getting a chauffeur's job." To **mitigate** is to soften, to make less harsh: "Because of the mitigating circumstances, the judge mitigated the lad's punishment. The sun's warmth soon mitigated our discomfort."

Oral/Written/Verbal— Strictly speaking, **oral** means "of the mouth, spoken," and **verbal** means "having to do with words—whether written or spoken." However, verbal has been used so often to mean "spoken" (as opposed to written) that good dictionaries recognize it as a fully legitimate usage. Recommendation: Use *oral* or *spoken* (rather than *verbal*) when talking about talking, *written* to mean words on paper. But don't criticize those who use *verbal* to mean *oral* or *spoken*.

Ordinance/Ordnance— An **ordinance** is a local law or regulation. **Ordnance** means military weapons, usually cannons or artillery.

Principle/Principal— A **principle** is a guiding rule (notice both end in -*le*), often a moral rule to live by. **Principal** means most important (the principal reason), the amount of a debt or investment (the payment includes principal and interest), someone authorized to conduct business (a meeting of principals only), the principal (chief executive) of the school staff.

Regime/Regimen— A **regime** (ruh ZHEEM) is a form of government, or the period of time a person or administration governs. "His regime was brutal." A

regimen (REDGE uh mun) is a set of rules or practices. "No dessert for me—I started my new health regimen yesterday."

Simple/Simplistic— Something **simple** can be good—a simple solution to a problem may be the best solution. But **simplistic** means unrealistically simple, oversimplified. In other words, someone who offers a simplistic solution probably doesn't understand the problem.

Sit/Set(and Lie/Lay, Rise/Raise)— The "i" words (sit, lie, rise) do NOT take objects. Their mates (set, lay, raise) do. Examples:
"Please sit. Set the book on the desk."
"I'm going to lie down. Lay the pillow on the bed."
"The smoke will rise. Let's raise the window."

Supersede (etc.)— Words ending in a "seed" sound are spelled three different ways: -cede, -ceed, and -sede.
One word, **supersede**, ends in -sede.
Three words, **succeed, proceed,** and **exceed,** end in -ceed. How to avoid a *speed*ing ticket? You'll *succeed* if you *proceed* without *exceed*ing the sp*eed* limit. Almost all the others end in -cede
(recede, concede, etc.).

Stationary/Stationery— This is simply (not simplistically) a spelling problem, and there's a simple solution. Notice the difference in spelling: station**a**ry means standing still, staying in one place. Station**e**ry is what we write letters on.

There/They're/Their— **There** means at that place: "She was there," or existence, "There are many confusing words." **They're** means they are: "They're good people." **Their** means belonging to them: "It's their car."

Two/To/Too— **Two** is a number. **To** is a preposition (to Virginia, to the end, to the store). **Too** means "also" or "excessively": "I'll come too, if that's not too many."

Your/You're— **Your** means "belonging to you." **You're** is a contraction meaning "you are."

"When I use a word, it means exactly what I want it to mean."
Humpty Dumpty

"If I…had words mean whatever I wanted them to mean…I would simply not be understood."
Kurt Vonnegut

Section 9 References

Where Do You Turn?

Writers and editors spend a lot of time looking up answers to questions. *The Landa List* will answer most of these, but some questions are outside its scope. Here are some often-used references (listed in alphabetical order by the names they're commonly called), with a short note about each. Remember, they're *guidebooks*, not *law books*. Read their advice, then do what you think works best for your own writing.

APA (*Publication Manual of the American Psychological Association*)

This book was originally intended as a guide for first-time writers of articles for psychological journals. It has become recognized as one of the best style manuals available, and is now commonly used by professional editors and writers in many fields.

AP Stylebook (*The Associated Press Stylebook and Libel Manual*)

Basically, a guide for journalists, newspaper editors, etc. This can be a good guide if you're writing a news release (e.g., about your organization).

Chicago (*The Chicago Manual of Style*)

A big book (more than 700 pages), and very comprehensive. It is an excellent manual for serious writers of nonfiction books, magazines, and certain nonbook items (like musical scores and poems). Learning to use it does takes a good deal of time and effort. (Suggestion: Use it for questions that don't come up very often, and put the answers in your own style sheet.)

Usage Dictionaries

Dictionary of English Usage, Dictionary of Problem Words and Expressions, etc. Usage dictionaries tell you what to do with troublesome terms and phrases. You should probably have access to one, but don't accept everything it says at face value. It was written by people like you and me, and we can choose to ignore its advice whenever we want.

Elements of Style

Strunk and White's book is popular and easy to read, but we think it's highly overrated. We haven't found it useful for answering specific questions.

GPO Style Manual

This one is often talked about, but rarely used by everyday writers and editors. Intended mainly as a guide for preparation of copy to be published by the Government Printing Office, it's hard to work with (you must spend time learning how it's organized), and rarely updated.

Landa List

A concise reference on some of the most-needed information about grammar, punctuation, spelling, and confusable words. Keep it handy, and use it often.

OED (*Oxford English Dictionary*)

A huge dictionary (the full version is 27 big volumes), it's the most thorough record of our language, and the only book that attempts to record every word in our language (and when the word first appeared in print). But even the OED is admittedly incomplete.

Roget's Thesaurus

A book of synonyms, it can help you find words with similar meanings. We keep one around, but almost never use it.

Style Manuals for Writing Theses, Term Papers, etc.

There are several of these, and your professor will probably tell you which to use. If not, (or if you're doing a report for work that's sort of academic), look through a few, select your own. Some of the most commonly used: Campbell's (*Form and Style in Thesis Writing*), Kate Turabian (*A Manual for Writers of Term Papers, Theses, and Dissertations*), MLA (*Handbook for Writers of Research Papers*).

Webster's New World Dictionary

WNWD is an excellent desk dictionary, as is *Webster's New Collegiate Dictionary*. Every writer and editor should keep a good desk dictionary within easy reach. **Note:** The name *Webster's* means nothing. Anyone can use it, and some clearly inferior books include it in their titles.

"Nobody can give you wiser advice than yourself."
Cicero

Index

A

abbreviations 6, 11
agreement
   pronoun-antecedent 25
   subject-verb 23
apostrophes
   abbreviations 6
   contractions 6
   names of organizations 6
   plurals 6
   possessive pronouns 6

B

brackets 15, 16
   in directions 16
   with quoted material 16
   within parentheses 16

C

capital letters 20
   don'ts 20
   geographical sections 20
   proper nouns 20
   titles 20
case 26
colons 8
   after salutation 8
   in chapter and verse 8
   in hours and minutes 8
   with quotations 8
   with series 8
commas 13
   after salutation 15
   don'ts 15
   in dates, places 14
   in numbers 15
   to prevent misreading 14
   to separate items in series 13
   to separate main clauses 13
   to set off nonessential elements 13
   with adjectives 14
   with direct quotations 14
   with interrupters 18
   with introductory words 13
   with inverted names 14
   with nouns of direct address 14
confusable words 39
conjunctions, pure 13
contractions 6

D

dashes
   before words that summarize 17
   with interrupters 18
double-bubble method 38

E

exclamation points 12
   after interjections 12

G

gender 25, 35
grammar 21
   active and passive sentences 24
   agreement: pronoun-antecedent 25
   agreement: subject-verb 23
   intransitive sentences 24, 25
   moods 29
   number 25
   parts of sentence 22
   parts of speech 21
   person 25

Q

question marks 12
  after direct questions 12
  in unlettered, unnumbered series 12
  to indicate uncertainty 12
quotation marks 8
  don'ts 10
  exact words 8
  parts of publications 9
  quotes with other marks 9
  words used in an unusual sense 9
  words, letters, numbers 9

R

references 43

S

semicolons 7
  and colons 7
  with series of items 7
spelling 31
  frequently misspelled words 34
  rules 31
subjunctive 29

T

titles
  capital letters in 20
  italics in 18
  quotation marks in 18
transitive sentences 24, 25

V

verbals 22

W

who/whom 27

Practice What You've Learned

Chatelaine Press offers three LandaBooks workbooks as companions to reinforce and expand the principles explained in *The Landa List*. Developed by the authors for their own teaching use, the workbooks are clear and easy for teachers and students to use.

The Wordsmith's Workbook

A collection of short exercises providing extensive practice in grammar and punctuation. Cumulative vocabulary drills teach commonly confused word pairs, and proofreading exercises home in on errors often overlooked. Contains pre- and post-tests. Teacher's guide available.

Writing That Works

Gives thorough discussion of organization and paragraphing, with suggested writing practice. Sentence exercises permit quick review of grammar and punctuation problems as needed. Teacher's guide available.

Building a Better Vocabulary

Studies show that vocabulary is highly related to career success, academic achievement, and IQ scores. This workbook covers common Latin and Greek roots and prefixes, as well as words clustered by the topics they describe (e.g., manias, hobbies, professions) and such commonly confused words as *affect* and *effect*. Stresses importance of context and mnemonics in learning words. Includes a section on using the dictionary (with its own pre-test). Pre- and post-tests included; teacher's guide available.

Also Available

Managing Other People's Writing

If you write in conjunction with others—whether as supervisor, team leader or member, or volunteer newsletter editor—you know how tricky a task you have. This little book can help you coordinate writing projects, avoid many problems, and better deal with the problems you can't prevent.